DR. RAY MALMASSARI

Cyber Warriors

Developing the Future of Cyber Professionals

A great leader doesn't only inspire us to have confidence in what THEY can do. A great leader inspires us to have confidence in what WE can do.

Simon Sinek

Contents

Preface

Cybersecurity is more than a profession; it is a calling. As the world becomes increasingly digital, the challenges we face in securing our systems, data, and infrastructure grow exponentially. The role of cybersecurity professionals—or cyber warriors—has never been more critical. It is their vigilance, creativity, and dedication that protect not only the technologies we rely on but also the trust and stability of modern society.

When I began my career in IT and cybersecurity over 15 years ago, I was driven by a passion for solving complex problems and a desire to protect what matters most. Along the way, I've had the privilege of mentoring talented individuals, leading resilient teams, and contributing to a field that is as dynamic as it is vital. Through these experiences, I've come to understand that cybersecurity is not just about tools and techniques—it's about people, purpose, and the willingness to adapt to an ever-changing landscape.

This book is a culmination of my journey, insights, and lessons learned. It is a guide for anyone who seeks to make an impact in cybersecurity, whether you are just starting out, transitioning into a leadership role, or looking to leave a legacy in the field. My hope is that this book will empower, inspire, and equip you to navigate the challenges and opportunities ahead.

The path of a cyber warrior is not without obstacles, but it is one of purpose and profound impact. Together, we can rise to meet the threats of today and build a safer digital future for tomorrow.

Disclaimer:

The views and opinions expressed in this content are solely those of Dr. Ray Malmassari and do not reflect or represent the views, policies, or positions of any organizations with which he is affiliated, including the Jacuzzi® Group. Mention of specific vendors or products does not constitute an endorsement or recommendation by any associated organization. All statements and opinions herein are made in a personal capacity.

1

Introduction

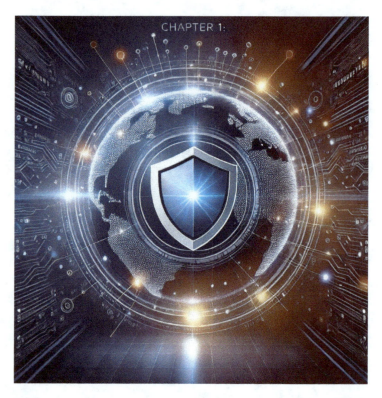

Cybersecurity is no longer a technical afterthought; it has become the foundation of modern society's infrastructure. Every industry, from healthcare to manufacturing, relies on interconnected systems and data to function effectively. With this dependence comes the growing need to safeguard against an ever-expanding range of cyber threats. As digital transformation accelerates, cybersecurity is not just about protecting assets—it's about preserving trust, ensuring privacy, and maintaining operational continuity.

The Evolution of Cybersecurity

Cybersecurity has evolved significantly over the past few decades. Initially, it was viewed as a niche field focused on securing isolated systems. However, the explosion of the internet and cloud technologies has shifted its importance. Today, cybersecurity encompasses protecting vast networks, sensitive data, and critical infrastructure.

Organizations are beginning to understand the stakes involved. According to a study by IBM, the average cost of a data breach in 2022 was $4.35 million. Beyond financial loss, these breaches erode consumer trust, damage reputations, and disrupt operations. The importance of cybersecurity is now widely recognized, but many organizations still struggle to prioritize it effectively.

Cybersecurity's Role in a Digital World

In my leadership role overseeing IT security and infrastructure for a global organization, I've witnessed firsthand the role cybersecurity plays in enabling innovation. Digitalization is a double-edged sword: it brings efficiency and growth opportunities but also exposes organizations to vulnerabilities. For example, when implementing Internet of Things (IoT) devices in a global manufacturing environment, security must be integrated into every stage—from design to deployment.

Leadership is a critical driver of cybersecurity success. Organizations with engaged leaders who invest in security initiatives tend to have a stronger security posture. During my doctoral research, I found that businesses that experienced a cyber incident were more likely to allocate resources to enhance their security measures. This underscores the importance of proactive leadership in preventing attacks rather than reacting to them.

Real-World Consequences of Cyber Neglect

The consequences of ignoring cybersecurity are well-documented. High-profile breaches, such as the SolarWinds attack and the Colonial Pipeline ransomware incident, demonstrate the far-reaching impact of cyber threats. These events disrupted supply chains, raised fuel prices, and triggered regulatory scrutiny.

Even smaller organizations are not immune. During my career, I've consulted for small businesses that underestimated their cyber risk until they became victims of ransomware. These incidents not only resulted in financial losses but also shook the confidence of their customers and partners.

Leadership Support: A Key Finding

One of the themes of my doctoral research is the critical role of leadership in cybersecurity. The research revealed that a lack of budget for technology and personnel is often a leadership and strategy issue, not just a financial one. Organizations must perceive cybersecurity as an enabler of business continuity rather than a cost center.

Effective leadership involves:

- **Championing Cybersecurity:** Leaders must advocate for security initiatives at the highest levels of the organization.
- **Allocating Resources:** Budgets for personnel, training, and technology must align with the organization's risk profile.
- **Building Awareness:** Leadership must foster a culture where cybersecurity is a shared responsibility.

Why Cybersecurity Matters to Everyone

Cybersecurity is not just an IT problem—it's a societal issue. From protecting personal privacy to securing national infrastructure, its importance cannot be overstated. As cyber warriors, we must educate others about the broader implications of our work.

For example, during the COVID-19 pandemic, cyberattacks targeting healthcare organizations surged. These attacks disrupted patient care, highlighting how cybersecurity failures can have life-or-death consequences. This underscores the need for every individual, regardless of their role, to understand and contribute to cybersecurity.

Call to Action

The rising importance of cybersecurity is a call to action for professionals, organizations, and governments alike. By prioritizing leadership support, investing in technology, and fostering a culture of security, we can build a safer digital future.

In this chapter, we've explored the evolution of cybersecurity and its growing importance in our interconnected world. In the next chapter, we'll delve deeper into the cyber threat landscape, examining the types of threats organizations face and how to prepare for them.

2

The Cyber Threat Landscape

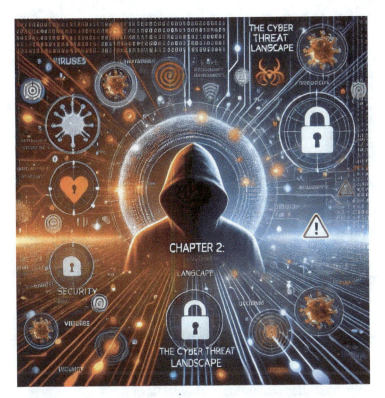

The cyber threat landscape is a constantly shifting battleground. As technology evolves, so do the methods and tactics employed by malicious actors. Organizations face threats ranging from ransomware and phishing attacks to nation-state espionage and insider risks. Understanding the threat landscape is essential for developing effective defenses and ensuring long-term resilience.

Types of Cyber Threats

To navigate this ever-changing environment, we must first identify the primary types of threats that organizations face:

Ransomware

Ransomware attacks have become one of the most pervasive and damaging forms of cyber threats. In these attacks, threat actors encrypt critical data and demand payment for its release. The Colonial Pipeline attack is a stark example of ransomware's impact, where operational shutdowns led to fuel shortages and economic disruption.

In my leadership role overseeing IT security and infrastructure for a global organization, I've dealt with organizations grappling with ransomware. One incident involved a small business that had not prioritized regular backups. When ransomware struck, they were left with no choice but to pay the ransom. This experience reinforced the importance of proactive measures, such as maintaining offline backups and conducting regular drills.

Phishing

Phishing remains one of the most common and effective attack vectors. These attacks involve tricking users into revealing sensitive information, such as passwords or financial data. Phishing is particularly dangerous because it targets human vulnerabilities rather than technical flaws.

During my doctoral research, I found that organizations with robust training programs had fewer incidents stemming from phishing. This highlights the importance of personnel training, a theme we'll revisit throughout this book.

Insider Threats

Insider threats occur when employees, contractors, or other trusted individuals misuse their access to harm the organization. These threats can be intentional (e.g., data theft) or unintentional (e.g., accidental leaks). Addressing insider threats requires a combination of technical controls, such as monitoring tools, and cultural strategies, such as fostering trust and accountability.

Nation-State Attacks

Nation-state actors target critical infrastructure, intellectual property, and government systems. These attacks are often sophisticated, leveraging zero-day vulnerabilities and advanced persistent threats (APTs). The SolarWinds breach is a prominent example, where attackers infiltrated multiple organizations using compromised software updates.

Organizations must adopt a proactive approach to defend against such threats, including threat intelligence sharing and collaboration with industry and government partners.

Key Insights from Research: The Role of Leadership

One of the key findings from my doctoral research is the relationship between leadership engagement and an organization's ability to address threats. Organizations that have experienced a cyber incident in the past are more likely to allocate resources toward improving their security posture. However, this reactive approach can be costly.

Proactive leadership involves:

- **Investing in Threat Intelligence:** Leadership must prioritize resources for monitoring and analyzing the threat landscape.
- **Promoting a Risk-Based Approach:** Security budgets should align with the organization's unique risk profile.
- **Encouraging Collaboration:** Effective leaders foster partnerships with external organizations to share insights and bolster defenses.

Organizations with engaged leaders are better equipped to adapt to the evolving threat landscape.

Emerging Threat Trends

The threat landscape continues to evolve, driven by advances in technology and shifting attacker motivations. Some emerging trends include:

Supply Chain Attacks

Supply chain attacks target third-party vendors or suppliers to compromise larger organizations. The Kaseya ransomware attack demonstrated the devastating impact of such tactics, affecting thousands of businesses worldwide. Organizations must vet their vendors rigorously and implement supply chain security measures.

IoT Vulnerabilities

The proliferation of Internet of Things (IoT) devices has expanded the attack surface for organizations. Many IoT devices lack robust security features, making them attractive targets. Securing IoT environments requires collaboration between manufacturers, users, and security professionals.

Artificial Intelligence (AI) in Cyberattacks

Threat actors are increasingly leveraging AI to enhance their attacks. AI-powered phishing campaigns, for example, can generate convincing messages tailored to individual targets. Defending against such attacks requires organizations to adopt AI-driven defenses.

Building Resilience: Strategies for Defense

To combat the threats outlined above, organizations must adopt a comprehensive defense strategy. Key components include:

Threat Intelligence

Threat intelligence involves gathering and analyzing data about potential threats to anticipate and mitigate attacks. Tools such as MITRE ATT&CK and government advisories provide valuable insights into attacker tactics.

Employee Training

As phishing and insider threats demonstrate, humans are often the weakest link in cybersecurity. Regular training on security best practices, coupled with simulations, can reduce the likelihood of successful attacks.

Incident Response Planning

A robust incident response plan ensures that organizations can detect, contain, and recover from incidents quickly. Regular tabletop exercises help teams prepare for real-world scenarios.

Zero Trust Architecture

Zero Trust Architecture (ZTA) eliminates the concept of implicit trust, requiring verification for every user and device. This approach minimizes the impact of insider threats and lateral movement within networks.

Real-World Case Study: Lessons from the SolarWinds Breach

The SolarWinds attack, one of the most significant breaches in recent history, highlights several lessons for navigating the threat landscape:

- **Importance of Vendor Management:** Organizations must assess and monitor their vendors' security practices.
- **Value of Threat Hunting:** Early detection of anomalies can prevent widespread damage.
- **Need for Collaboration:** Sharing insights across industries can enhance collective defense.

These lessons demonstrate that navigating the threat landscape requires a proactive and collaborative approach.

Call to Action

The cyber threat landscape is vast and dynamic, but understanding its key components is the first step toward effective defense. By investing in leadership, fostering collaboration, and staying informed about emerging trends, organizations can build resilience against even the most sophisticated threats.

In the next chapter, we'll shift our focus to the individuals who defend against these threats: cyber warriors. We'll explore the skills, knowledge, and mindset required to succeed in this critical role.

3

The Path to Becoming a Cyber Warrior

The journey to becoming a cyber warrior is one of continuous learning, practical experience, and personal growth. Cyber warriors are the first line of defense against digital threats, and the demand for skilled professionals in this field has never been higher. This chapter serves as a roadmap for individuals seeking to enter or advance in the cybersecurity field, providing guidance on acquiring skills, building a professional network, and cultivating the mindset required for success.

Defining the Cyber Warrior

Cyber warriors are more than technical experts; they are

problem solvers, innovators, and leaders. They embody a unique combination of skills and attributes, including:

- **Technical Proficiency:** A deep understanding of systems, networks, and security principles.
- **Adaptability:** The ability to learn and apply new tools and techniques quickly.
- **Critical Thinking:** The capacity to analyze complex situations and develop effective solutions.
- **Resilience:** The determination to persist in the face of challenges and setbacks.

During my career, I've mentored numerous individuals transitioning into cybersecurity. One of the key lessons I've emphasized is that success in this field requires a commitment to lifelong learning and a willingness to embrace challenges.

Building Foundational Skills

Every cyber warrior's journey begins with a solid foundation of technical skills. These skills serve as the building blocks for more advanced knowledge and specialization.

Networking and Systems Administration

A strong understanding of how networks and systems operate is essential for identifying and mitigating vulnerabilities. Key topics to explore include:

- TCP/IP protocols
- Firewalls and routers
- Operating systems (Windows, Linux, macOS)

Programming and Scripting

Basic programming and scripting skills enable cyber warriors to automate tasks, analyze malware, and develop custom tools. Recommended languages include:

- Python: Ideal for automating tasks and conducting security testing.
- Bash: Useful for scripting in Unix/Linux environments.
- JavaScript: Commonly used in web application security.

Cybersecurity Basics

Familiarity with fundamental cybersecurity concepts is critical. These include:

- Encryption and cryptography
- Risk management frameworks
- Incident response processes

Many free and affordable online resources, such as Coursera, Cybrary, and YouTube tutorials, are available to help aspiring professionals develop these skills.

Certifications: Validating Expertise

Certifications are a valuable way to demonstrate knowledge and expertise. They serve as industry-recognized credentials that open doors to new opportunities. Below is a suggested certification pathway based on experience levels:

Beginner-Level Certifications

- **CompTIA Security+:** Covers basic security concepts, tools, and practices.
- **Certified Ethical Hacker (CEH):** Focuses on penetration

testing and ethical hacking fundamentals.
- **Cisco CyberOps Associate:** Introduces concepts of security operations centers (SOCs) and threat analysis.

Intermediate-Level Certifications

- **Certified Information Systems Auditor (CISA):** Focuses on auditing and assessing security systems.
- **Offensive Security Certified Professional (OSCP):** A hands-on certification for penetration testing.
- **Certified Information Security Manager (CISM):** Emphasizes security management.

Advanced-Level Certifications

- **Certified Information Systems Security Professional (CISSP):** A globally recognized certification covering various domains of security.
- **Certified Chief Information Security Officer (CCISO):** Prepares professionals for leadership roles.
- **GIAC Security Expert (GSE):** An advanced certification for seasoned professionals.

Certifications are not only a mark of credibility but also an opportunity to gain in-depth knowledge through structured learning.

Gaining Practical Experience

Hands-on experience is essential for bridging the gap between theory and practice. Here are some ways to gain practical experience in cybersecurity:

Home Labs

Setting up a home lab is one of the most effective ways to practice skills. Tools like VirtualBox, Kali Linux, and Wireshark allow you to simulate real-world scenarios in a safe environment.

Capture The Flag (CTF) Competitions

CTF events challenge participants to solve security-related puzzles, such as reverse engineering, cryptography, and penetration testing. These competitions are a great way to develop technical skills and network with other professionals.

Internships and Volunteer Work

Internships provide invaluable exposure to real-world environments. Volunteering for open-source projects or nonprofit organizations is another way to gain experience while giving back to the community.

Bug Bounty Programs

Platforms like HackerOne and Bugcrowd allow individuals to identify and report vulnerabilities in exchange for rewards. Bug bounty programs offer hands-on experience with real-world systems and applications.

Building a Professional Network

Networking is a crucial component of career growth. A strong professional network provides access to job opportunities, mentorship, and collaborative learning.

Industry Events

Conferences like DEF CON, Black Hat, and RSA are excellent opportunities to meet industry leaders and learn about the latest trends. Virtual events and webinars have also become popular, making it easier to connect with others from anywhere in the world.

Online Communities

Forums and social media platforms, such as LinkedIn, Reddit (e.g., r/cybersecurity), and Discord, host active cybersecurity communities. Engaging in these spaces allows you to exchange ideas, ask questions, and build relationships.

Mentorship

Mentorship is one of the most effective ways to accelerate personal and professional growth. During my career, I've seen how guidance from experienced professionals can help individuals navigate challenges and reach their full potential. Seek out mentors who align with your goals and values.

Cultivating the Cyber Warrior Mindset

Beyond technical skills, a successful cyber warrior possesses a growth-oriented mindset. Key aspects include:

Curiosity

Stay curious and eager to learn. Cybersecurity is a field that rewards those who explore new technologies and delve into complex problems.

Resilience

The journey is not without setbacks. Whether it's a failed certification exam or a challenging project, resilience will keep you moving forward.

Integrity

Cyber warriors must uphold the highest ethical standards. Trust is the foundation of this profession, and maintaining it is paramount.

Call to Action

Becoming a cyber warrior is a journey of continuous learning and growth. By building foundational skills, gaining hands-on experience, and cultivating a strong network, you can carve out a meaningful and impactful career in cybersecurity.

In the next chapter, we'll explore how to foster a cybersecurity culture within organizations, ensuring that security becomes a shared responsibility at every level.

4

Building a Cybersecurity Culture

Technology alone cannot secure an organization. The strongest defenses come from a combination of tools, processes, and—most importantly—people. A cybersecurity culture is the foundation of any successful security strategy, ensuring that everyone in the organization, from entry-level employees to senior executives, is aligned with the goal of protecting critical assets. This chapter explores the role of leadership, training, and governance in fostering a culture where cybersecurity is a shared responsibility.

The Role of Leadership in Cybersecurity Culture

Leadership is the driving force behind any organizational culture, and cybersecurity is no exception. Leaders set the tone for how security is perceived and prioritized. Without visible support from the top, even the best policies and tools are likely to fail.

Leading by Example

Executives and managers must model the behaviors they want to see in their teams. For example, if leaders adhere to password policies and participate in security training, employees are more likely to follow suit.

In my leadership role overseeing IT security and infrastructure, I prioritized leading by example to inspire and guide my team. When implementing new security measures, I personally ensured my adherence to the same standards required of my teams. This approach reinforced the importance of accountability and fairness in driving cultural change.

Communicating the Why

Employees are more likely to embrace security practices when they understand their purpose. Leadership should communicate how cybersecurity aligns with the organization's mission and values. For instance, in industries like healthcare, emphasizing the role of security in protecting patient data can foster a stronger commitment to compliance.

Training and Awareness: Empowering the Workforce

A cybersecurity culture is built on the foundation of an informed and empowered workforce. Employees are often the first line of defense against threats like phishing and social engineering. Providing them with the knowledge and tools to recognize and respond to risks is essential.

Tailored Training Programs

Training should be tailored to the unique needs and roles of employees. For example:

- **Frontline Staff:** Focus on identifying phishing attempts, securing endpoints, and reporting incidents.
- **IT Teams:** Cover advanced topics like patch management, threat detection, and incident response.
- **Executives:** Highlight the financial, legal, and reputational risks associated with cyber incidents.

During my doctoral research, I found that organizations with robust, role-specific training programs experienced fewer incidents caused by human error. This underscores the importance of customizing training to ensure relevance and engagement.

Gamification of Training

Gamification is an effective way to make training more engaging and impactful. Incorporating elements like quizzes, simulations, and leaderboards can motivate employees to actively participate. For example, phishing simulations can be gamified by rewarding teams that achieve the highest detection rates.

Measuring Effectiveness

Training programs must be evaluated regularly to ensure they are achieving their objectives. Metrics such as the number of reported phishing attempts, employee participation rates, and post-training assessment scores can provide valuable insights into the program's effectiveness.

Governance and Processes: The Backbone of Culture

Strong governance ensures that cybersecurity practices are embedded into the organization's operations. Governance involves establishing policies, procedures, and frameworks that guide behavior and decision-making.

Establishing Clear Policies

Policies should be clear, concise, and accessible to all employees. Examples include acceptable use policies, data classification guidelines, and incident reporting procedures. Policies should be reviewed and updated regularly to reflect changes in technology and regulations.

Integrating Security into Business Processes

Cybersecurity should not be an afterthought. It must be integrated into every business process, from product development to vendor selection. For example, implementing secure development practices in software projects can reduce vulnerabilities and lower remediation costs.

Promoting Accountability

Accountability is key to maintaining a cybersecurity culture. Establishing roles and responsibilities ensures that everyone understands their part in protecting the organization. For example:

- IT teams are responsible for implementing technical controls.
- Employees are responsible for following security policies.
- Executives are responsible for allocating resources and overseeing governance.

Overcoming Challenges to Building a Cybersecurity Culture

Creating a cybersecurity culture is not without challenges. Resistance to change, competing priorities, and limited resources can hinder progress. However, these challenges can be overcome with the right strategies:

Addressing Resistance to Change

Resistance often stems from a lack of understanding or fear of added complexity. Leadership should focus on education and communication to address these concerns. For example, demonstrating how security measures simplify processes (e.g., single sign-on) can help gain buy-in.

Balancing Security and Usability

Security measures must strike a balance between protection and usability. Overly restrictive controls can frustrate employees and lead to non-compliance. In my experience, involving end users in the design and implementation of security measures can help address this challenge.

Securing Budget and Resources

Limited budgets are a common obstacle to fostering a cybersecurity culture. My research revealed that organizations with proactive leadership are more likely to allocate resources to security initiatives. Building a strong business case that highlights the financial and reputational costs of a breach can help secure funding.

Example Scenario: Building a Cybersecurity Culture in a Manufacturing Organization

In a mid-sized manufacturing organization, a ransomware attack exposed the need for a stronger cybersecurity culture. Initially, employees perceived security as solely the responsibility of the IT department, and compliance with security practices was minimal.

To address this challenge, the organization implemented the

following steps:

1. **Engaged Leadership:** Conducted workshops with executives to align security with business goals.
2. **Developed Training Programs:** Introduced role-specific training with simulations to increase awareness.
3. **Integrated Governance:** Established clear policies and integrated security into operational processes.

Within a year, the organization saw a significant reduction in phishing incidents and improved compliance with security protocols. This example highlights the importance of leadership and collaboration in fostering a robust cybersecurity culture.

Call to Action

Building a cybersecurity culture is an ongoing effort that requires leadership, training, and governance. By empowering employees, integrating security into business processes, and overcoming challenges, organizations can create a culture where cybersecurity becomes second nature.

In the next chapter, we'll discuss how to navigate the evolving threat landscape and develop strategies for staying ahead of emerging risks.

5

Navigating the Threat Landscape

The cybersecurity threat landscape is a constantly evolving battlefield. To stay ahead of adversaries, organizations must not only understand the threats they face but also develop proactive strategies to identify, mitigate, and respond to risks. This chapter explores the importance of a risk-based approach, the role of leadership in prioritizing security, and actionable strategies for navigating today's complex cyber threat environment.

Understanding Risk in the Threat Landscape

Cybersecurity is not a one-size-fits-all endeavor. Each organization has a unique risk profile based on factors such as its industry, size, and regulatory requirements. For example, financial institutions face significant risks related to fraud and data theft, while healthcare organizations are particularly vulnerable to ransomware attacks due to their reliance on operational uptime.

Risk Assessment

A comprehensive risk assessment is the foundation of any effective cybersecurity strategy. This process involves:

- Identifying assets, such as data, systems, and infrastructure, that need protection.
- Assessing potential threats, including external actors (e.g., hackers, nation-states) and internal risks (e.g., insider threats, accidental errors).
- Evaluating vulnerabilities in existing systems and processes.

During my career, I've conducted numerous risk assessments for organizations of all sizes. One critical lesson I've learned is the importance of involving stakeholders from across the organization to ensure all risks are considered.

Risk Prioritization

Not all risks are created equal. A risk-based approach prioritizes addressing the most critical vulnerabilities based on their likelihood and potential impact. Tools like risk matrices can help organizations allocate resources effectively.

Leadership's Role in Navigating Risks

Leadership is crucial in navigating the threat landscape. Organizations with engaged leaders are better equipped to anticipate and respond to emerging threats.

Aligning Security with Business Goals

Effective leaders ensure that cybersecurity aligns with the organization's broader objectives. For example, a retail company prioritizing e-commerce growth must address risks related to payment security and data privacy.

Fostering a Proactive Mindset

Proactive leaders invest in measures that prevent attacks rather than simply reacting to incidents. During my doctoral research, I found that organizations that experienced a cyber incident in the past were more likely to allocate resources to security. However, adopting a proactive approach can save time, money, and reputation.

Strategies for Navigating the Threat Landscape

Organizations can navigate the threat landscape effectively by adopting a combination of technical controls, employee training, and continuous monitoring. Below are some key strategies:

Implementing Threat Intelligence

Threat intelligence involves gathering and analyzing information about potential threats to make informed decisions. Examples of threat intelligence platforms include:

- **MITRE ATT&CK:** A framework for understanding adversary tactics and techniques.
- **AlienVault:** A tool for aggregating threat data and automating analysis.

By leveraging threat intelligence, organizations can anticipate attacks and take preventive measures. For example, identifying phishing campaigns targeting the industry can help refine email security protocols.

Adopting Zero Trust Architecture

Zero Trust Architecture (ZTA) is based on the principle of "never trust, always verify." This approach minimizes risks by requiring verification for every user and device, regardless of their location. Key components of ZTA include:

- Multi-factor authentication (MFA)
- Micro-segmentation of networks
- Continuous monitoring of user behavior

During my tenure, implementing elements of Zero Trust significantly reduced the risk of insider threats and unauthorized access.

Regularly Testing Defenses

Penetration testing and vulnerability assessments are essential for identifying weaknesses in defenses. These tests simulate real-world attacks to evaluate the effectiveness of security measures. Organizations should conduct these tests regularly and prioritize addressing high-risk vulnerabilities.

Emerging Threats and Challenges

The threat landscape is constantly evolving, driven by advancements in technology and changes in attacker behavior. Below are some of the emerging threats and challenges organizations must prepare for:

Supply Chain Attacks

Supply chain attacks target third-party vendors to compromise larger organizations. The SolarWinds breach is a notable example, where attackers infiltrated multiple companies through compromised software updates. Organizations must vet their vendors carefully and establish robust supply chain security measures.

Ransomware-as-a-Service

Ransomware has become a business model for cybercriminals, with ransomware-as-a-service (RaaS) platforms enabling even inexperienced actors to launch attacks. Defending against ransomware requires robust backup strategies, endpoint detection, and user training.

Deepfakes and AI-Driven Attacks

Advances in artificial intelligence (AI) have enabled attackers to create convincing deepfake videos, audio, and images. These tools can be used for social engineering, disinformation campaigns, and financial fraud. Organizations must invest in AI-driven defenses to counter these threats.

Example Scenario: Combating Phishing Attacks

Phishing is one of the most prevalent and effective attack methods due to its simplicity. Consider a mid-sized organization that experienced a phishing campaign targeting employees with fake emails disguised as HR announcements, leading to multiple compromised accounts.

To address this, the following measures were implemented:

1. **Enhanced Email Security:** Added filtering tools to identify and block phishing emails.
2. **Employee Training:** Conducted phishing simulations to educate employees on recognizing and reporting suspicious emails.
3. **Incident Response Playbooks:** Developed clear procedures for isolating and addressing compromised accounts.

Within six months, the organization saw a significant reduction in successful phishing attempts, demonstrating the value of a multi-layered approach.

Monitoring and Adapting to the Landscape

Navigating the threat landscape is not a one-time effort. Organizations must continuously monitor their environment and adapt to new challenges. This involves:

- **Staying Informed:** Following industry news, threat intelligence feeds, and government advisories.
- **Collaborating:** Sharing insights and best practices with peers and industry groups.
- **Evolving:** Regularly updating policies, tools, and training programs to address emerging risks.

Call to Action

The threat landscape is vast and dynamic, but it is not insurmountable. By adopting a proactive, risk-based approach and leveraging the right tools and strategies, organizations can stay ahead of adversaries. Leadership, collaboration, and continuous improvement are key to navigating this ever-changing environment.

In the next chapter, we'll explore the role of technology in cyber defense, examining the tools and innovations that empower organizations to protect themselves against advanced threats.

6

The Role of Technology in Cyber Defense

Technology is at the heart of modern cybersecurity. It enables organizations to detect, prevent, and respond to threats in ways that were unimaginable just a few decades ago. However, technology alone is not enough; it must be implemented thoughtfully, integrated with organizational processes, and supported by leadership. This chapter explores the tools and innovations that form the backbone of cyber defense and provides guidance on how to maximize their effectiveness.

The Foundations of Cyber Defense Technology

At its core, cybersecurity technology is designed to achieve three main objectives:

1. **Prevention:** Blocking threats before they cause harm.
2. **Detection:** Identifying suspicious activity or breaches as they occur.
3. **Response:** Mitigating damage and restoring normal operations after an incident.

To achieve these objectives, organizations must implement a layered approach to security, commonly referred to as defense-in-depth. This involves deploying multiple tools and technologies across different levels of the organization's infrastructure.

Key Cyber Defense Tools and Technologies

Below are some of the most critical tools in the cybersecurity arsenal, along with practical advice for their implementation:

Firewalls

Firewalls act as the first line of defense by monitoring and controlling incoming and outgoing network traffic. Modern firewalls, such as Next-Generation Firewalls (NGFWs), offer advanced features like intrusion prevention systems (IPS) and deep packet inspection (DPI).

Best Practices for Firewalls:

- Regularly update firewall rules to reflect changes in the network.
- Implement segmentation to isolate sensitive systems from less critical ones.
- Monitor firewall logs for unusual activity.

Endpoint Detection and Response (EDR)

Endpoints, such as laptops, desktops, and mobile devices, are common entry points for attackers. EDR solutions monitor endpoint activity, detect threats, and respond to incidents in real time.

During my tenure with a global organization, deploying EDR tools allowed us to identify and neutralize malware before it could spread. The ability to quarantine infected endpoints remotely was particularly valuable for a distributed workforce.

Security Information and Event Management (SIEM)

SIEM systems collect and analyze log data from across the organization to provide a centralized view of security events. They use correlation rules and machine learning to detect anomalies and alert security teams.

Benefits of SIEM:

- Improved visibility into network activity.
- Faster detection of advanced threats.
- Simplified compliance reporting.

Identity and Access Management (IAM)

IAM solutions ensure that only authorized individuals can access systems and data. Key components include multi-factor authentication (MFA), single sign-on (SSO), and role-based access control (RBAC).

One of the insights from my doctoral research was the importance of IAM in preventing insider threats. By enforcing least-privilege access, organizations can limit the potential damage caused by compromised accounts.

Threat Intelligence Platforms

Threat intelligence platforms aggregate data about emerging threats and vulnerabilities, enabling organizations to stay ahead of attackers. Examples include Recorded Future, ThreatConnect, and Open Threat Exchange.

Use Case: During a consulting engagement with a healthcare provider, we integrated a threat intelligence platform to identify and block phishing campaigns targeting their industry. This proactive approach reduced the number of successful attacks significantly.

Emerging Technologies in Cyber Defense

The cybersecurity landscape is continually evolving, and new technologies are emerging to address the latest challenges. Below are some of the most promising innovations:

Artificial Intelligence (AI) and Machine Learning (ML)

AI and ML are transforming cybersecurity by enabling faster and more accurate threat detection. For example:

- AI-driven tools can analyze vast amounts of data to identify patterns indicative of an attack.
- ML algorithms can adapt to new threats without manual intervention.

Quantum Cryptography

As quantum computing becomes more accessible, traditional encryption methods may become vulnerable. Quantum cryptography offers a way to secure communications against quantum attacks by leveraging the principles of quantum mechanics.

Zero Trust Architecture (ZTA)

Zero Trust eliminates implicit trust within networks, requiring verification for every user and device. Key technologies that support ZTA include software-defined perimeters (SDPs) and continuous monitoring tools.

Challenges in Implementing Technology

While technology is a powerful enabler, its implementation is not without challenges. Below are some common obstacles and strategies to overcome them:

Budget Constraints

Many organizations struggle to secure funding for advanced cybersecurity tools. My research revealed that budgets often increase after an incident, but proactive investment is more cost-effective.

Solution: Build a strong business case by quantifying the potential financial and reputational impact of a breach. Highlight how technology can reduce costs in the long term by preventing incidents.

Integration Issues

Integrating new tools with existing systems can be complex and time-consuming. This is particularly true in organizations with legacy infrastructure.

Solution: Choose tools that are compatible with your current environment and involve cross-functional teams in the implementation process.

Skills Gaps

The effectiveness of cybersecurity technology depends on the skills of those managing it. However, many organizations face a shortage of qualified professionals.

Solution: Invest in training and development programs to upskill your workforce. Partnering with Managed Security Service Providers (MSSPs) can also fill gaps temporarily.

Example Scenario: Strengthening Endpoint Security in a Hybrid Work Environment

In a manufacturing organization transitioning to a hybrid

work model, securing remote endpoints posed a significant challenge. Employees frequently used personal devices, which increased the organization's attack surface.

To address this, the following measures were implemented:

1. **Deploying EDR:** An endpoint detection and response (EDR) solution was deployed to monitor all devices accessing the network, ensuring continuous protection.
2. **Training Employees:** Employees received training to identify and report suspicious activity, fostering awareness and proactive behavior.
3. **Policy Enforcement:** Strict policies were enforced, allowing only authorized devices to access company resources, reducing the risk of unauthorized access.

Outcome: Within three months, the organization experienced a significant reduction in malware infections and unauthorized access attempts, demonstrating the effectiveness of a comprehensive approach to endpoint security in a hybrid work environment.

Maximizing the Impact of Cyber Defense Technology

To get the most out of cybersecurity tools, organizations should:

- **Adopt a Holistic Approach:** Technology should complement people and processes.
- **Continuously Evaluate Effectiveness:** Regularly review and update tools to address evolving threats.
- **Leverage Automation:** Automation can help reduce the workload on security teams by handling repetitive tasks

like log analysis.

Call to Action

Technology is a critical enabler of cybersecurity, but its success depends on thoughtful implementation, continuous evaluation, and leadership support. By leveraging the right tools and strategies, organizations can build a robust defense against even the most advanced threats.

In the next chapter, we'll focus on the art of incident response, exploring how organizations can prepare for, respond to, and recover from cyber incidents.

7

The Art of Incident Response

CHAPTER 7: THE ART OF
INCIDENT RESPONSE

In cybersecurity, incidents are not a question of if but when. No organization is immune to cyber threats, which makes a robust incident response strategy a cornerstone of any cybersecurity program. The ability to detect, respond to, and recover from incidents swiftly can mean the difference between a minor disruption and a full-blown crisis. This chapter explores the key components of effective incident response, the role of leadership, and lessons learned from real-world scenarios.

What is Incident Response?

Incident response is a structured approach to managing

and mitigating the impact of cybersecurity incidents. These incidents can range from malware infections and phishing attacks to data breaches and denial-of-service (DoS) attacks.

The primary objectives of incident response are to:

1. **Limit Damage:** Contain the incident to prevent further harm.
2. **Restore Operations:** Resume normal activities as quickly as possible.
3. **Learn and Improve:** Identify lessons learned to enhance future preparedness.

A well-designed incident response plan ensures that everyone in the organization knows their role and responsibilities during a crisis.

The Incident Response Lifecycle

The National Institute of Standards and Technology (NIST) outlines a four-phase incident response lifecycle that serves as a framework for managing incidents effectively:

Preparation

Preparation is the foundation of incident response. Organizations must develop and test their response capabilities before an incident occurs.

Key activities include:

- Developing an incident response plan (IRP) that outlines roles, responsibilities, and procedures.
- Establishing a communication plan to ensure timely and accurate information sharing.
- Conducting regular training and simulations to build team

readiness.

During my tenure with a global manufacturing organization, we conducted annual tabletop exercises to simulate various incident scenarios. These exercises helped identify gaps in our processes and improved team coordination.

Detection and Analysis

The detection phase involves identifying potential incidents through monitoring and alerts. Analysis determines the scope, impact, and nature of the incident.

Best practices for detection include:

- Implementing tools like SIEM systems and intrusion detection systems (IDS).
- Training employees to recognize and report suspicious activity.
- Using threat intelligence feeds to stay informed about emerging threats.

Containment, Eradication, and Recovery

Once an incident is confirmed, the priority is to contain it to prevent further damage. This is followed by eradicating the threat and recovering affected systems.

Steps include:

- **Containment:** Isolate infected systems or segments of the network.
- **Eradication:** Remove malware, close vulnerabilities, and clean up affected systems.
- **Recovery:** Restore operations using backups and ensure systems are fully secured before bringing them back online.

For example, during a ransomware attack on a client organization, we isolated the affected servers, restored data from offline backups, and applied patches to prevent reinfection. This swift response minimized downtime and financial losses.

Post-Incident Activity

The final phase involves reviewing the incident to identify lessons learned and improve the response plan.

Activities include:

- Conducting a post-incident review to evaluate the effectiveness of the response.
- Updating policies, procedures, and tools based on findings.
- Sharing insights with stakeholders to enhance organizational awareness.

The Role of Leadership in Incident Response

Leadership plays a critical role in incident response by ensuring that the organization is prepared, supported, and aligned during a crisis.

Building a Response Team

An effective response requires a multidisciplinary team, often referred to as a Computer Security Incident Response Team (CSIRT). The CSIRT should include representatives from IT, legal, communications, and executive leadership.

Securing Resources

Leadership must allocate the necessary resources for incident response, including tools, training, and personnel. My doctoral research revealed that organizations with proactive leadership are better equipped to handle incidents due to their investment in preparation.

Maintaining Communication

Clear and transparent communication is essential during an incident. Leadership must manage both internal and external communications to ensure consistency and accuracy.

Example Scenario: Mitigating a Phishing Attack

A financial organization experienced a phishing attack that compromised several employee accounts. The outdated incident response plan resulted in delays in containment, exacerbating the damage caused by the attack.

Key actions taken to resolve the incident:

1. **Immediate Containment:** Disabled the compromised accounts and reset passwords to prevent further access.
2. **Incident Analysis:** Identified the phishing email and blocked similar messages from reaching employees.
3. **Plan Updates:** Revised the incident response plan to include clear, actionable steps for handling phishing incidents.

Outcome: Following the incident, the organization conducted additional phishing simulations and enhanced its email security measures. These improvements significantly reduced the likelihood of future phishing attacks and strengthened overall resilience.

Incident Response Tools and Resources

Several tools and frameworks can enhance an organization's incident response capabilities:

- **Playbooks:** Predefined workflows for common incident

types, such as ransomware or data breaches.
- **Forensic Tools:** Software like EnCase and FTK for analyzing digital evidence.
- **Frameworks:** NIST's Cybersecurity Framework and SANS Incident Response Process provide guidelines for best practices.

Challenges in Incident Response

Despite its importance, incident response is not without challenges. Common obstacles include:

- **Lack of Preparation:** Many organizations fail to develop or test their response plans.
- **Skills Gaps:** Responding to complex incidents requires specialized expertise, which is often in short supply.
- **Resource Constraints:** Limited budgets can hinder the acquisition of tools and training.

To overcome these challenges, organizations should prioritize preparation, invest in training, and consider partnerships with external incident response providers.

Building Resilience Through Incident Response

Incident response is not just about reacting to incidents; it's about building resilience. Organizations that can recover quickly from incidents are better positioned to maintain trust and minimize long-term impact.

Steps to enhance resilience include:

1. **Conducting Regular Drills:** Simulate real-world scenarios

to test and improve response capabilities.

2. **Integrating Business Continuity Planning:** Align incident response with broader continuity and disaster recovery efforts.

3. **Fostering a Culture of Security:** Empower employees to recognize and report incidents, reducing response times.

Call to Action

Incident response is both an art and a science. By preparing in advance, leveraging the right tools, and fostering collaboration across teams, organizations can navigate incidents with confidence and efficiency. Leadership support and continuous improvement are essential for turning lessons learned into actionable strategies.

In the next chapter, we'll explore ethical hacking and penetration testing—essential practices for identifying vulnerabilities and strengthening defenses.

8

Ethical Hacking and Penetration Testing

In the world of cybersecurity, one of the best ways to strengthen defenses is to think like an attacker. Ethical hacking and penetration testing allow organizations to uncover vulnerabilities, test their defenses, and identify gaps before malicious actors exploit them. These practices not only enhance an organization's security posture but also build resilience by simulating real-world attack scenarios. This chapter dives into the methodologies, tools, and benefits of ethical hacking and penetration testing while addressing the importance of leadership support for such initiatives.

What is Ethical Hacking?

Ethical hacking involves using the same techniques and tools as malicious hackers, but with the organization's permission and for the purpose of improving security. Ethical hackers, often referred to as "white-hat hackers," aim to identify vulnerabilities, report them to the organization, and provide recommendations for remediation.

Key principles of ethical hacking include:

1. **Permission:** Ethical hackers must obtain explicit authorization before testing systems.
2. **Purpose:** The goal is to improve security, not to cause harm or disrupt operations.
3. **Confidentiality:** Ethical hackers must protect the data they access during testing.

During my time in cybersecurity leadership, I've seen firsthand how ethical hacking can uncover critical vulnerabilities that would have otherwise gone unnoticed. For example, penetration testing of a web application revealed misconfigured permissions that allowed unauthorized data access. Addressing this issue before a breach occurred saved the organization significant costs and reputational damage.

The Penetration Testing Process

Penetration testing, or "pen testing," is a controlled simulation of an attack on an organization's systems. The goal is to identify vulnerabilities and assess the effectiveness of existing security measures. The process typically involves five key phases:

Planning and Reconnaissance

In this phase, testers gather information about the target environment. This includes:

- Identifying IP addresses, domains, and subdomains.
- Mapping the organization's network and infrastructure.
- Collecting data on potential vulnerabilities.

Tools like Nmap and Shodan are often used during reconnaissance.

Scanning

Scanning involves actively probing systems to identify weaknesses. For example:

- **Network Scanning:** Detecting open ports and services.
- **Vulnerability Scanning:** Identifying known vulnerabilities using tools like Nessus or OpenVAS.

Gaining Access

This phase simulates an attacker's efforts to exploit vulnerabilities and gain access to systems. Techniques may include:

- Exploiting software vulnerabilities.
- Using stolen credentials obtained through phishing simulations.
- Leveraging misconfigurations in cloud environments.

Maintaining Access

Testers assess whether they can maintain access to compromised systems. This phase helps evaluate the organization's ability to detect and respond to breaches.

Analysis and Reporting

The final phase involves documenting findings, including vulnerabilities discovered, data accessed, and the impact of potential exploitation. The report should include clear recommendations for addressing the issues.

Types of Penetration Testing
Penetration testing can target various aspects of an organization's environment. Common types include:

Network Penetration Testing
Focuses on identifying vulnerabilities in network infrastructure, such as firewalls, routers, and wireless networks.

Web Application Testing
Evaluates the security of web applications by testing for issues like SQL injection, cross-site scripting (XSS), and insecure authentication mechanisms.

Social Engineering Testing
Assesses the organization's ability to resist social engineering attacks, such as phishing or pretexting. This often involves simulating phishing campaigns to test employee awareness.

Physical Penetration Testing
Tests the security of physical premises, such as server rooms or data centers, by attempting unauthorized access.

Tools for Ethical Hacking and Penetration Testing
Ethical hackers use a wide range of tools to simulate attacks and identify vulnerabilities. Some of the most popular tools include:

- **Kali Linux:** A Linux distribution designed specifically for penetration testing, with pre-installed tools like Metasploit and Wireshark.

- **Burp Suite:** A tool for testing web applications, particularly useful for identifying vulnerabilities like XSS and SQL injection.
- **Metasploit Framework:** An open-source tool for developing and executing exploit code.
- **OWASP ZAP:** A web application security scanner that helps identify common vulnerabilities.
- **John the Ripper:** A password-cracking tool used to test password strength.

During my career, I've worked with penetration testers who used these tools to uncover vulnerabilities ranging from weak passwords to unpatched software. These findings often led to significant improvements in the organization's security posture.

Leadership's Role in Ethical Hacking Initiatives

Leadership plays a crucial role in supporting ethical hacking and penetration testing initiatives. Without leadership buy-in, these activities may face resistance or be deprioritized due to perceived risks or costs.

Securing Budget and Resources

Penetration testing can be resource-intensive, requiring skilled professionals and advanced tools. Leadership must allocate sufficient budget to ensure these initiatives are conducted effectively.

Establishing Clear Objectives

Leaders should define the goals of penetration testing, such as identifying vulnerabilities in critical systems or assessing compliance with regulations.

Promoting Transparency

Ethical hacking activities should be transparent and well-communicated to stakeholders. Employees, for example, should understand the purpose of simulated phishing campaigns to avoid unnecessary anxiety.

Encouraging a Proactive Mindset

Leadership should view ethical hacking as a proactive measure to prevent incidents rather than a reactive response to past breaches.

Challenges and Ethical Considerations

While ethical hacking offers significant benefits, it is not without challenges and ethical concerns. Common issues include:

- **Scope Creep:** Testing activities that go beyond the agreed-upon scope can lead to unintended consequences.
- **Data Privacy:** Testers must handle sensitive data responsibly to avoid exposing it during testing.
- **False Positives:** Misinterpreting results can lead to unnecessary remediation efforts.

To address these challenges, organizations should work with qualified professionals and establish clear rules of engagement.

Example Scenario: Enhancing Web Application Security

A financial technology startup discovered vulnerabilities in their web application during a penetration test. These included improper input validation and weak encryption of sensitive data, which could have been exploited to gain unauthorized access to customer accounts.

Actions Taken:

1. **Addressed Input Validation Issues**: Resolved improper input validation to prevent SQL injection attacks.
2. **Upgraded Encryption Protocols**: Improved encryption standards to secure sensitive customer data.
3. **Implemented Logging and Monitoring**: Added robust logging and monitoring capabilities to detect and respond to future attacks.

Outcome: The organization successfully passed a third-party security audit, increasing trust among investors and customers and solidifying their reputation for strong security practices.

Benefits of Ethical Hacking and Penetration Testing

The value of ethical hacking extends beyond identifying vulnerabilities. Benefits include:

- **Enhanced Security:** Strengthening defenses before attackers exploit vulnerabilities.
- **Regulatory Compliance:** Meeting the requirements of frameworks like GDPR, HIPAA, and PCI-DSS.
- **Increased Awareness:** Educating employees and stakeholders about potential risks.
- **Improved Resilience:** Building confidence in the organization's ability to withstand attacks.

Call to Action

Ethical hacking and penetration testing are essential components of a robust cybersecurity strategy. By simulating real-world attacks, organizations can uncover weaknesses, strengthen defenses, and build resilience. Leadership support, skilled professionals, and the right tools are key to maximizing the benefits of these initiatives.

In the next chapter, we'll shift our focus to the future of cybersecurity, exploring emerging trends and technologies that will shape the field in the years to come.

9

The Future of Cybersecurity

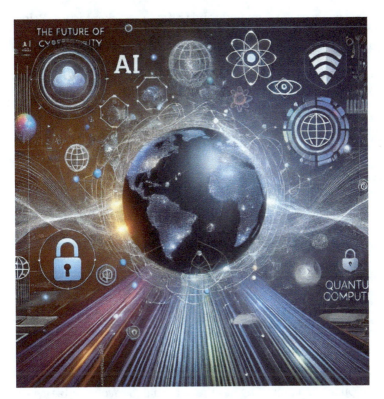

The future of cybersecurity is shaped by a rapidly evolving threat landscape, technological advancements, and the growing interconnectivity of the digital world. As cyber threats become more sophisticated, organizations must adopt forward-thinking strategies to stay ahead of adversaries. In this chapter, we will explore emerging trends, technologies, and challenges that will define the future of cybersecurity, and discuss how organizations and professionals can adapt to these changes.

Emerging Trends in Cybersecurity

The cybersecurity landscape is constantly changing, driven

by advances in technology and shifts in attacker tactics. Below are some of the key trends shaping the future of the field:

The Rise of Artificial Intelligence (AI) in Cybersecurity

AI and machine learning are transforming the way organizations detect and respond to cyber threats. These technologies enable faster analysis of vast amounts of data, allowing for more accurate threat detection and response. For example:

- AI-driven security tools can identify anomalies in network traffic that may indicate an attack.
- Machine learning algorithms can predict future threats based on historical data.

However, AI is a double-edged sword. While it empowers defenders, attackers are also leveraging AI to create more sophisticated phishing campaigns, automate attacks, and evade detection. Organizations must invest in AI-driven tools while remaining vigilant against AI-powered threats.

Quantum Computing and Its Implications for Encryption

Quantum computing has the potential to revolutionize cybersecurity, but it also poses significant risks. Quantum computers could break traditional encryption algorithms, rendering many current security measures obsolete. To prepare for this, organizations should:

- Explore quantum-safe encryption methods, such as lattice-based cryptography.
- Monitor developments in post-quantum cryptography standards.

Increased Focus on Zero Trust Architecture

The shift toward Zero Trust Architecture (ZTA) is becoming more prevalent as organizations recognize the limitations of perimeter-based security models. ZTA requires continuous verification of users and devices, regardless of their location. Key components of ZTA include:

- Identity and access management (IAM)
- Network segmentation
- Continuous monitoring of user behavior

The Impact of IoT and 5G

The Internet of Things (IoT) and 5G networks are expanding the attack surface for organizations. While these technologies bring significant benefits, they also introduce new security challenges:

IoT Vulnerabilities

IoT devices often lack robust security features, making them attractive targets for attackers. For example, insecure IoT devices can be used to launch Distributed Denial-of-Service (DDoS) attacks. Organizations must:

- Implement strong access controls for IoT devices.
- Regularly update firmware to address vulnerabilities.
- Segment IoT networks to limit the impact of a breach.

5G Security Challenges

5G networks enable faster data transfer and increased connectivity, but they also introduce new risks, such as:

- Increased reliance on software-based network functions,

which may have vulnerabilities.
- Greater potential for supply chain attacks targeting 5G infrastructure.

To address these challenges, organizations should collaborate with telecom providers to ensure secure deployment and operation of 5G networks.

Cybersecurity Talent and Workforce Challenges

The cybersecurity skills gap continues to be a significant challenge. As demand for skilled professionals grows, organizations must find innovative ways to attract, retain, and develop talent.

Upskilling the Workforce

Organizations should invest in training programs to upskill their current employees. For example:

- Offer courses on emerging technologies like AI and cloud security.
- Provide hands-on experience through labs and simulations.

Encouraging Diversity in Cybersecurity

A diverse workforce brings unique perspectives and problem-solving approaches. Efforts to increase diversity in cybersecurity include:

- Creating mentorship programs for underrepresented groups.
- Partnering with educational institutions to promote cybersecurity careers.

Leveraging Automation

To address the skills gap, organizations can use automation to handle routine tasks, allowing human analysts to focus on more complex challenges. Tools like Security Orchestration, Automation, and Response (SOAR) platforms streamline incident response and threat hunting.

Cyber Resilience: Preparing for the Unknown

The concept of cyber resilience goes beyond traditional cybersecurity. It emphasizes the ability to anticipate, withstand, and recover from cyber incidents. Key aspects of cyber resilience include:

Proactive Threat Hunting

Threat hunting involves actively searching for indicators of compromise (IoCs) within networks. This proactive approach helps organizations detect threats that may bypass traditional security measures.

Business Continuity Planning

Cyber resilience requires integrating cybersecurity with broader business continuity and disaster recovery plans. This ensures that critical operations can continue even during a cyber crisis.

Collaboration and Information Sharing

Sharing threat intelligence with industry peers and government agencies enhances collective defense. For example, platforms like the Information Sharing and Analysis Centers (ISACs) provide valuable insights into emerging threats.

Leadership in the Future of Cybersecurity

Leadership will play a pivotal role in shaping the future of cybersecurity. Proactive leaders must:

- **Prioritize Innovation:** Encourage the adoption of new technologies while addressing associated risks.
- **Foster a Culture of Security:** Ensure that cybersecurity is a shared responsibility across the organization.
- **Invest in Talent Development:** Support continuous learning and professional growth for cybersecurity teams.

During my doctoral research, I found that leadership engagement significantly impacts an organization's ability to adapt to evolving threats. Organizations with forward-thinking leaders are better positioned to navigate the challenges of the future.

Example Scenario: Preparing for Post-Quantum Security

A financial institution initiated efforts to assess the potential impact of quantum computing on its encryption protocols and proactively strengthen its security posture.

Key Actions Taken:

1. **Evaluating Current Cryptographic Methods:** Identified areas where current encryption methods could be vulnerable to quantum computing capabilities.
2. **Testing Quantum-Safe Algorithms:** Experimented with post-quantum cryptography to ensure compatibility with existing systems while maintaining robust security.
3. **Developing a Transition Plan:** Created a detailed roadmap for migrating to quantum-resistant encryption standards, ensuring a smooth transition over time.

Outcome: This proactive approach positioned the institution as a leader in quantum security preparedness, enhancing both its resilience and customer trust in its ability to protect sensitive data.

Call to Action

The future of cybersecurity is filled with both challenges and opportunities. By embracing emerging technologies, fostering innovation, and prioritizing talent development, organizations can build a resilient security posture that adapts to the demands of tomorrow.

In the next chapter, we'll explore the qualities and strategies required to become a leader in cybersecurity, focusing on how to inspire and guide teams to achieve excellence.

10

Becoming a Leader in Cybersecurity

Leadership in cybersecurity is about more than managing teams and processes—it's about inspiring others, driving innovation, and fostering a culture of resilience in the face of evolving threats. Whether you are stepping into a leadership role for the first time or looking to refine your approach, effective leadership in cybersecurity requires a unique blend of technical expertise, strategic vision, and emotional intelligence.

This chapter explores the qualities and strategies that define successful cybersecurity leaders and provides actionable guidance on how to lead teams to excellence.

The Role of Leadership in Cybersecurity

Cybersecurity leaders are tasked with navigating complex challenges while balancing the needs of their teams, organizations, and stakeholders. Their role involves:

1. **Setting the Vision:** Defining the organization's cybersecurity goals and aligning them with business objectives.
2. **Empowering Teams:** Equipping team members with the resources, skills, and confidence they need to succeed.
3. **Driving Innovation:** Encouraging the adoption of new technologies and approaches to stay ahead of adversaries.
4. **Ensuring Accountability:** Establishing clear roles and responsibilities to maintain focus and discipline.

Throughout my career, I've learned that effective leadership is not about having all the answers—it's about creating an environment where others feel empowered to contribute and innovate.

Qualities of an Effective Cybersecurity Leader

Successful cybersecurity leaders share certain traits that enable them to navigate the complexities of the field. These qualities include:

Emotional Intelligence

Emotional intelligence (EQ) is the ability to understand and manage your own emotions while empathizing with others. In cybersecurity, where high-stress situations are common, EQ is essential for:

- Building strong relationships with team members and stakeholders.

- Managing conflicts and resolving disagreements construc-
tively.
- Maintaining composure during incidents and crises.

Adaptability

The cybersecurity landscape is constantly evolving, and leaders must be able to adapt to new threats, technologies, and
regulations. This requires a willingness to:

- Embrace change and encourage innovation within the team.
- Stay informed about emerging trends and best practices.
- Pivot strategies when circumstances demand it.

Strategic Thinking

Cybersecurity leaders must balance immediate concerns with
long-term goals. Strategic thinking involves:

- Assessing risks and prioritizing resources effectively.
- Aligning cybersecurity initiatives with the organization's
mission and objectives.
- Anticipating future challenges and opportunities.

Communication Skills

Clear and effective communication is critical for leaders,
especially when explaining complex technical concepts to non-
technical audiences. Leaders must:

- Translate technical risks into business terms that executives
can understand.
- Foster open communication within the team to encourage
collaboration and knowledge sharing.

- Advocate for cybersecurity initiatives at all levels of the organization.

Strategies for Leadership Success

Leadership in cybersecurity is as much about mindset and approach as it is about technical expertise. Below are some strategies for excelling as a cybersecurity leader:

Foster a Collaborative Culture

Collaboration is key to solving complex security challenges. As a leader, you can encourage collaboration by:

- Creating opportunities for cross-functional teams to work together on security initiatives.
- Promoting knowledge sharing through regular meetings, workshops, and documentation.
- Recognizing and celebrating team achievements to boost morale.

During my tenure with a global manufacturing organization, I established a cybersecurity steering committee that included representatives from IT, legal, and operations. This cross-functional approach helped align security efforts with broader business goals.

Invest in Continuous Learning

The cybersecurity field evolves rapidly, and leaders must stay ahead of the curve. Encourage both personal and team growth by:

- Attending industry conferences and webinars to stay informed about emerging trends.

- Providing training opportunities for team members to develop new skills.
- Leading by example by pursuing advanced certifications or participating in professional development programs.

Delegate Effectively

Delegation is not about offloading tasks—it's about empowering team members to take ownership of their responsibilities. Effective delegation involves:

- Clearly defining roles and expectations.
- Trusting team members to make decisions within their areas of expertise.
- Providing guidance and support when needed.

Delegation also allows leaders to focus on strategic priorities while enabling team members to grow and develop.

Cultivate Resilience

Resilience is the ability to recover from setbacks and adapt to challenges. In cybersecurity, where incidents are inevitable, resilience is critical for both leaders and teams. You can cultivate resilience by:

- Encouraging a growth mindset that views failures as opportunities for learning.
- Building strong relationships within the team to foster trust and mutual support.
- Establishing clear incident response protocols to minimize uncertainty during crises.

Leadership Challenges and How to Overcome Them

Cybersecurity leaders face unique challenges that require thoughtful solutions. Below are some common challenges and strategies for addressing them:

Gaining Executive Buy-In

Convincing executives to invest in cybersecurity can be challenging, especially when budgets are tight. To gain buy-in:

- Speak the language of business by framing cybersecurity as a risk management and value-adding function.
- Use data to demonstrate the potential impact of threats and the ROI of security initiatives.
- Highlight success stories from other organizations to illustrate the benefits of proactive investment.

Balancing Technical and Managerial Responsibilities

Cybersecurity leaders often find themselves juggling technical and managerial roles. To strike a balance:

- Delegate technical tasks to trusted team members where possible.
- Set aside time for strategic planning and leadership development.
- Focus on building a team that can operate independently while keeping you informed.

Managing Stress and Burnout

The high-pressure nature of cybersecurity can take a toll on leaders. To manage stress:

- Practice self-care and encourage your team to do the same.

- Delegate responsibilities to avoid overburdening yourself.
- Seek support from mentors, peers, or professional networks.

Real-World Example: Building a High-Performing Cybersecurity Team

While leading a global cybersecurity team, I prioritized creating an environment where team members felt empowered to take initiative. This involved:

1. **Establishing Clear Goals:** Defined key performance indicators (KPIs) aligned with organizational objectives.
2. **Promoting Professional Growth:** Provided team members with opportunities to pursue certifications and attend conferences.
3. **Fostering Open Communication:** Encouraged team members to share ideas and feedback without fear of judgment.

The result was a high-performing team that consistently exceeded expectations, even in the face of challenging incidents.

Call to Action

Becoming a leader in cybersecurity requires more than technical expertise—it demands emotional intelligence, strategic thinking, and a commitment to fostering collaboration and growth. By embracing these qualities and strategies, you can inspire your team, drive innovation, and create a lasting impact in the field.

In the next chapter, we'll discuss the importance of continuous learning and professional growth in cybersecurity, and how staying ahead of the curve can benefit both individuals and organizations.

11

Continuous Learning and Professional Growth

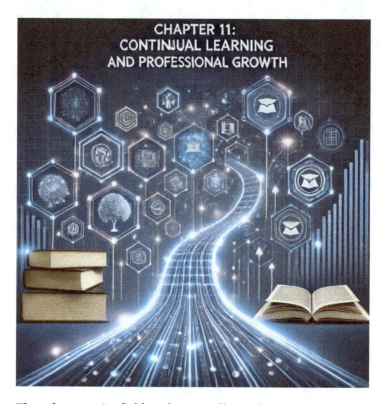

The cybersecurity field evolves rapidly, with new threats, technologies, and regulations emerging almost daily. Professionals who thrive in this industry understand that continuous learning and development are essential for staying ahead. This chapter explores the importance of ongoing education, practical strategies for professional growth, and the benefits of embracing a lifelong learning mindset.

Why Continuous Learning Matters

The dynamic nature of cybersecurity demands that professionals remain adaptable and informed. Key reasons for prioritizing continuous learning include:

Keeping Up with Evolving Threats

Cybercriminals constantly develop new tactics, techniques, and procedures (TTPs). Staying updated on the latest threats ensures that you can defend against them effectively.

Adapting to New Technologies

Emerging technologies such as artificial intelligence (AI), blockchain, and quantum computing are transforming cybersecurity. Understanding these technologies enables professionals to leverage them for defense and identify potential vulnerabilities.

Meeting Regulatory Requirements

Governments and industries frequently update cybersecurity regulations and standards. Continuous learning ensures compliance and avoids penalties.

Building a Continuous Learning Plan

A structured approach to learning can help you stay focused and achieve your professional goals. Below are some steps to create an effective learning plan:

Assess Your Current Skills

Start by identifying your strengths and areas for improvement. Consider seeking feedback from colleagues, mentors, or supervisors to gain additional insights.

Set Specific Goals

Define clear, measurable objectives for your learning journey. For example:

- Obtain a specific certification, such as CISSP or OSCP.
- Gain proficiency in a new programming language, such as Python.

- Stay informed about developments in a niche area, such as cloud security or threat intelligence.

Leverage Multiple Learning Resources

Continuous learning involves exploring various educational resources, including:

- **Online Courses:** Platforms like Udemy, Pluralsight, and Cybrary offer cybersecurity courses on a wide range of topics.
- **Books and Publications:** Stay informed by reading books, whitepapers, and industry reports.
- **Podcasts and Webinars:** Podcasts such as "The CyberWire" and "SANS Internet Storm Center" provide insights into current trends and developments.

Allocate Dedicated Time

Set aside regular time for learning, whether it's a few hours each week or a portion of your daily routine. Consistency is key to making progress.

Certifications: A Stepping Stone to Growth

Certifications validate your knowledge and expertise, opening doors to new opportunities. Below are some popular certifications for different stages of your cybersecurity career:

Beginner-Level Certifications

- **CompTIA Security+:** Covers fundamental security concepts and practices.
- **Certified Ethical Hacker (CEH):** Focuses on penetration testing and ethical hacking basics.

- **Cisco Certified CyberOps Associate:** Introduces concepts of threat analysis and SOC operations.

Intermediate-Level Certifications

- **Certified Information Systems Auditor (CISA):** Emphasizes auditing and assessing security systems.
- **GIAC Certified Incident Handler (GCIH):** Covers incident response and threat hunting.
- **Offensive Security Certified Professional (OSCP):** A hands-on certification for penetration testing.

Advanced-Level Certifications

- **Certified Information Systems Security Professional (CISSP):** A globally recognized credential for security management.
- **Certified Chief Information Security Officer (CCISO):** Prepares professionals for executive leadership roles.
- **GIAC Security Expert (GSE):** An elite certification for advanced professionals.

Networking and Mentorship

Building relationships with other professionals in the field is a powerful way to accelerate growth and stay informed about industry trends.

Networking Opportunities

Engage with the cybersecurity community through:

- **Conferences:** Events like Black Hat, DEF CON, and RSA are

excellent for networking and learning.
- **Online Communities:** Platforms like LinkedIn, Reddit (e.g., r/cybersecurity), and Discord host active cybersecurity discussions.
- **Local Meetups:** Join local cybersecurity groups or chapters of professional organizations like (ISC)^2 or ISACA.

Mentorship

Mentorship provides valuable guidance and support for your career. As both a mentor and mentee, I've experienced the transformative impact of these relationships. Seek mentors who align with your goals and are willing to share their expertise. Additionally, consider mentoring others to solidify your knowledge and give back to the community.

Staying Resilient in Your Career Journey

The cybersecurity field can be demanding, with high-pressure situations and constant challenges. Building resilience is critical for long-term success.

Embrace a Growth Mindset

View challenges and failures as opportunities to learn and improve. This mindset fosters adaptability and perseverance.

Prioritize Self-Care

Maintaining your mental and physical well-being is essential. Take breaks, set boundaries, and engage in activities outside of work to recharge.

Celebrate Progress

Acknowledge and celebrate your achievements, no matter how small. This reinforces motivation and builds confidence.

Real-World Example: Pursuing Continuous Learning in Lead-

ership

When I transitioned into a leadership role within a global organization, I realized that my technical expertise alone was not enough to succeed. To grow as a leader, I pursued certification CCISO, which built upon the knowledge of the CISSP, attended leadership workshops, and sought mentorship from experienced executives, CIOs and CISOs.

This commitment to continuous learning allowed me to:

- Communicate more effectively with stakeholders.
- Align cybersecurity initiatives with business objectives.
- Empower my team to achieve their full potential.

The Role of Organizations in Supporting Growth

Organizations play a crucial role in fostering continuous learning among their employees. Leaders should:

- **Provide Training Opportunities:** Offer access to courses, workshops, and certifications.
- **Encourage Knowledge Sharing:** Create platforms for employees to share insights and best practices.
- **Recognize Achievements:** Celebrate employees' accomplishments to reinforce a culture of growth.

Call to Action

Continuous learning is not just a career strategy—it's a mindset that enables you to adapt, thrive, and lead in the ever-changing field of cybersecurity. By setting clear goals, leveraging diverse resources, and embracing challenges, you can achieve personal and professional growth while staying ahead of emerging threats.

In the next chapter, we'll explore how to build a legacy in cybersecurity, focusing on mentorship, innovation, and contributions to the broader community.

12

Building a Legacy in Cybersecurity

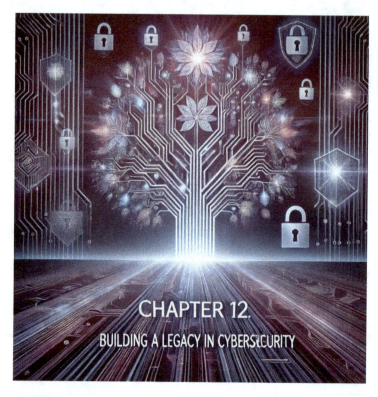

CHAPTER 12.
BUILDING A LEGACY IN CYBERSECURITY

Building a legacy in cybersecurity is about more than achieving personal success; it's about making a lasting impact on the field and inspiring future generations. Whether through mentorship, innovation, or contributions to the broader cybersecurity community, a meaningful legacy reflects the values and dedication of a true cyber warrior. In this chapter, we explore how to leave a positive and enduring mark on the cybersecurity profession.

The Importance of Building a Legacy

Why does leaving a legacy matter? In cybersecurity, the threats we face evolve rapidly, and the skills, knowledge, and inspiration we pass on can empower others to continue the fight. A legacy is not only a testament to individual achievements but also a way to strengthen the profession as a whole.

Key reasons to focus on building a legacy include:

1. **Mentorship:** Guiding and inspiring the next generation of professionals.
2. **Innovation:** Advancing the field through research, tools, and frameworks.
3. **Community Impact:** Contributing to the collective knowledge and resilience of the cybersecurity community.

During my career, I've experienced the profound impact of mentors and thought leaders who shaped my journey. Their guidance and example motivated me to pursue excellence and pay it forward.

Mentorship: Guiding the Next Generation

Mentorship is one of the most powerful ways to leave a legacy. By sharing your knowledge and experience, you can help others navigate challenges, achieve their goals, and unlock their potential.

Becoming a Mentor

Becoming a mentor involves more than offering advice—it's about building meaningful relationships and empowering others to succeed. Key principles of effective mentorship include:

- **Active Listening:** Understand your mentee's aspirations, challenges, and needs.
- **Providing Guidance:** Share your experiences and insights

while encouraging independent thinking.
- **Offering Support:** Celebrate successes, provide constructive feedback, and be a source of encouragement.

Finding Mentorship Opportunities

Opportunities to mentor others exist in many forms, including:

- Formal mentorship programs within organizations or professional associations.
- Informal relationships with colleagues or community members.
- Online platforms and forums where you can connect with aspiring professionals.

As a mentor, I've found great satisfaction in helping individuals transition into cybersecurity leadership roles. Seeing their growth and contributions to the field reinforces the value of mentorship.

Driving Innovation and Advancing the Field

Innovation is at the heart of cybersecurity. By creating new tools, frameworks, or methodologies, you can address emerging challenges and enhance the profession's capabilities.

Conducting Research

Research is a critical component of advancing cybersecurity. Whether through academic studies or industry-driven initiatives, research can uncover valuable insights and solutions. For example:

- My doctoral research highlighted the importance of lead-

ership support, compliance, and training in improving organizational security posture.
· Findings from this research have informed strategies for small businesses to enhance their defenses.

Developing Tools and Frameworks

Creating practical tools or frameworks can make a significant impact. For instance:

· Open-source projects, such as vulnerability scanners or threat intelligence platforms, benefit the community by providing accessible resources.
· Frameworks like the NIST Cybersecurity Framework offer structured approaches to managing security risks.

Promoting Collaboration

Collaboration is essential for driving innovation. Engage with industry peers, government agencies, and academic institutions to share knowledge and tackle complex challenges collectively.

Contributing to the Cybersecurity Community

Giving back to the cybersecurity community is another way to build a lasting legacy. Contributions can take many forms, including:

· **Publishing Articles and Thought Leadership:** Share your expertise through articles, blogs, or presentations at conferences. Platforms like LinkedIn, Medium, and industry journals provide opportunities to reach a wide audience.
· **Hosting Workshops and Webinars:** Educate others by hosting sessions on topics ranging from incident response

to emerging technologies.

- **Participating in Open-Source Projects:** Collaborate on initiatives that benefit the community, such as developing security tools or frameworks.

During my career, I've contributed to the community through publications, educational content on YouTube, and consulting services via CyCure Solutions. These efforts aim to empower businesses and professionals with the knowledge and tools needed to succeed in cybersecurity.

Inspiring Future Leaders

A true legacy inspires others to continue the journey and drive progress. This involves:

- **Fostering Leadership Skills:** Encourage others to develop the qualities and capabilities needed for leadership roles.
- **Advocating for Diversity and Inclusion:** Promote initiatives that ensure cybersecurity is accessible to individuals from all backgrounds.
- **Celebrating Achievements:** Recognize and celebrate the accomplishments of colleagues and community members to inspire ongoing excellence.

One of my proudest achievements has been mentoring team members who have gone on to lead their own cybersecurity initiatives. Seeing their success reinforces the importance of supporting and empowering future leaders.

Example Scenario: Creating Lasting Impact Through Collaboration

A healthcare organization partnered with its IT team to develop a comprehensive cybersecurity training program aimed at enhancing employee awareness. The program's success not only improved internal security practices but also became a model adopted by other organizations in the industry.

Key elements of the program included:

1. **Role-Specific Training**: Tailored training for different employee groups to address their specific cybersecurity responsibilities.
2. **Phishing Simulations**: Conducted regular simulations to test and improve employees' ability to recognize and respond to phishing attempts.
3. **Continuous Improvement**: Established a feedback loop to refine the program based on participant insights and evolving cybersecurity threats.

Outcome: The success of this initiative highlighted the value of collaboration and knowledge sharing in creating a sustainable and positive impact on cybersecurity awareness across industries.

The Ripple Effect of Legacy

A meaningful legacy extends beyond individual contributions. It creates a ripple effect, inspiring others to pursue excellence, innovate, and give back to the community. By focusing on mentorship, innovation, and community engagement, you can leave a legacy that continues to benefit the field for years to come.

Call to Action

Building a legacy in cybersecurity is a lifelong journey that requires passion, dedication, and a commitment to making a difference. Whether you mentor others, drive innovation, or contribute to the community, your efforts will shape the future of the field and inspire the next generation of cyber warriors.

In the next chapter, we'll conclude with a reflection on the journey of a cyber warrior and a call to action for individuals and organizations to rise to the challenges of the future.

13

The Journey Ahead

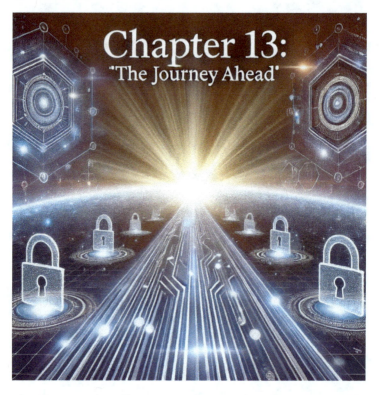

The journey of a cyber warrior is one of purpose, resilience, and continuous growth. As technology advances and the world becomes increasingly interconnected, the challenges in cybersecurity will only grow more complex. However, these challenges also present opportunities to make a meaningful impact, protect what matters most, and shape a safer digital future.

This final chapter reflects on the journey of a cyber warrior, offers guidance for staying motivated, and calls on individuals and organizations to rise to the challenges of the future.

Reflecting on the Journey

The path of a cyber warrior is not a straightforward one. It is filled with challenges, lessons, and triumphs that shape both personal and professional growth. Reflecting on this journey helps us appreciate the progress we've made and the contributions we've made to the field.

Overcoming Challenges

Every cyber warrior faces obstacles, from technical hurdles to resource constraints. These challenges test our skills, patience, and determination. However, they also provide opportunities to learn and grow.

For example, during my career, I've encountered incidents where the odds seemed stacked against us—ransomware attacks, insider threats, and more. In each case, the collaborative efforts of my team and our ability to adapt allowed us to overcome these challenges and emerge stronger.

Celebrating Successes

Success in cybersecurity is not just about preventing breaches—it's about building trust, enabling innovation, and creating a culture of security. Celebrating these successes, both big and small, reinforces the value of our work and inspires others to strive for excellence.

Staying Motivated for the Future

Cybersecurity can be a demanding field, but it is also incredibly rewarding. Staying motivated is essential for maintaining resilience and enthusiasm throughout your career.

Finding Purpose

Understanding the broader impact of your work can provide a sense of purpose. As cyber warriors, we protect not only systems and data but also the people and communities that rely on them. This sense of purpose can drive us to continue learning, innovating, and pushing boundaries.

Focusing on Growth

Cybersecurity is a journey of continuous improvement. Embrace opportunities to learn new skills, take on challenging projects, and expand your horizons. Personal growth is one of the most fulfilling aspects of this profession.

Building a Support Network

Surround yourself with mentors, peers, and colleagues who share your passion for cybersecurity. A strong support network can provide encouragement, guidance, and collaboration opportunities.

A Call to Action for Cyber Warriors

The future of cybersecurity depends on the collective efforts of individuals, organizations, and governments. As cyber warriors, we have a responsibility to rise to the challenges of the future and make a lasting impact.

For Individuals

Whether you are an aspiring professional, an experienced practitioner, or a leader, there are steps you can take to contribute to the field:

- Pursue continuous learning and stay informed about emerging threats and technologies.
- Mentor others and share your knowledge to inspire the next generation of cyber warriors.
- Advocate for a culture of security within your organization and community.

For Organizations

Organizations play a critical role in shaping the cybersecurity landscape. Leaders and decision-makers must:

- Invest in the tools, training, and personnel needed to build robust defenses.
- Foster collaboration across teams and with external partners to strengthen resilience.
- Promote diversity and inclusion to ensure a wide range of perspectives in tackling cybersecurity challenges.

For Governments and Industry Leaders

Policymakers and industry leaders must work together to:

- Develop and enforce regulations that protect critical infrastructure and sensitive data.
- Encourage public-private partnerships to share threat intelligence and resources.
- Support initiatives that address the cybersecurity skills gap and promote workforce development.

The Legacy of a Cyber Warrior

The impact of a cyber warrior extends far beyond their individual contributions. By protecting systems, mentoring others, and driving innovation, we leave behind a legacy of resilience, trust, and inspiration.

As I reflect on my own journey, I am reminded of the mentors, colleagues, and experiences that shaped my path. The lessons I've learned and the relationships I've built have reinforced my commitment to making a difference in this field. I encourage you to do the same—to embrace the challenges, celebrate the successes, and strive to leave a lasting impact.

Looking Ahead: The Journey Continues

The journey of a cyber warrior is never truly complete. As technology evolves and new challenges arise, there will always be opportunities to grow, learn, and contribute. Whether you are just starting out or are a seasoned professional, your journey matters. Your efforts protect not only the digital world but also the trust and well-being of society as a whole.

The future of cybersecurity is in our hands. Together, we can rise to the challenges, embrace the opportunities, and build a safer digital future for generations to come.

Final Call to Action

Cyber warriors, the journey ahead is full of challenges, but it is also rich with opportunities to make a difference. Take the knowledge, insights, and inspiration from this book and use them to shape your path, empower others, and contribute to the greater good. The world needs your vigilance, creativity, and dedication. Rise to the occasion and leave a legacy that inspires future generations.

About the Author

Dr. Ray Malmassari is a seasoned cybersecurity and IT professional with over 15 years of experience in the field and a passion for empowering others to succeed. He currently serves as the Head of IT Security and Infrastructure at Jacuzzi® Group, where he leads global teams, mentors rising professionals, and oversees critical aspects of IT strategy and security operations.

Earning the rank of Eagle Scout was the cornerstone of Dr. Malmassari's career and ambitions, instilling in him the values of dedication, leadership, and perseverance that have guided his professional journey. With advanced degrees in Information Technology, including a recently completed Doctorate in IT specializing in Cybersecurity, Dr. Malmassari brings a wealth of expertise and insight to the table. He holds industry-recognized certifications such as CISSP, CCISO, CNDA, and PMP, showcasing his technical proficiency and leadership capabilities.

Dr. Malmassari is also the CEO and Founder of CyCure Solutions, an IT and cybersecurity consulting firm dedicated to empowering small and medium-sized businesses with strategic solutions and robust security frameworks.

Dr. Malmassari's doctoral research focused on critical themes in small business cybersecurity, revealing key insights that are vital for organizations aiming to enhance their security posture:

Leadership Support for Enhancing Security Posture with Technology and Personnel: His research highlighted that a lack of budget for personnel and technology is often a leadership challenge. Budgets tend to increase when the perceived threat of a cyber incident rises, especially in organizations with past incidents.

Industry Compliance with Regulations: Effective compliance requires leadership to invest adequately in governance and align financial investments with security goals.

Personnel Security Awareness and Training: He emphasized the importance of training personnel on technology and cyber-security best practices while continually evaluating training effectiveness.

Beyond his professional accomplishments, Dr. Malmassari shares his expertise through his YouTube channel, where he creates educational content on IT and cybersecurity. His articles, published in leading industry outlets, further establish him as a thought leader committed to advancing the field.

When he's not safeguarding digital frontiers or mentoring others, Dr. Malmassari enjoys exploring the intersection of technology and strategy, solving Rubik's cubes in under two minutes, and traveling to gain new perspectives. His life's mission is to leave a legacy of resilience, trust, and inspiration in the cybersecurity field. Feel free to connect with him on LinkedIn.

You can connect with me on:

- https://www.linkedin.com/in/raymalmassari
- https://www.youtube.com/@cybersageray
- http://www.cycuresolutions.com